GOPHER

BAROQUE

AND

OTHER

BEASTLY

CONCEITS

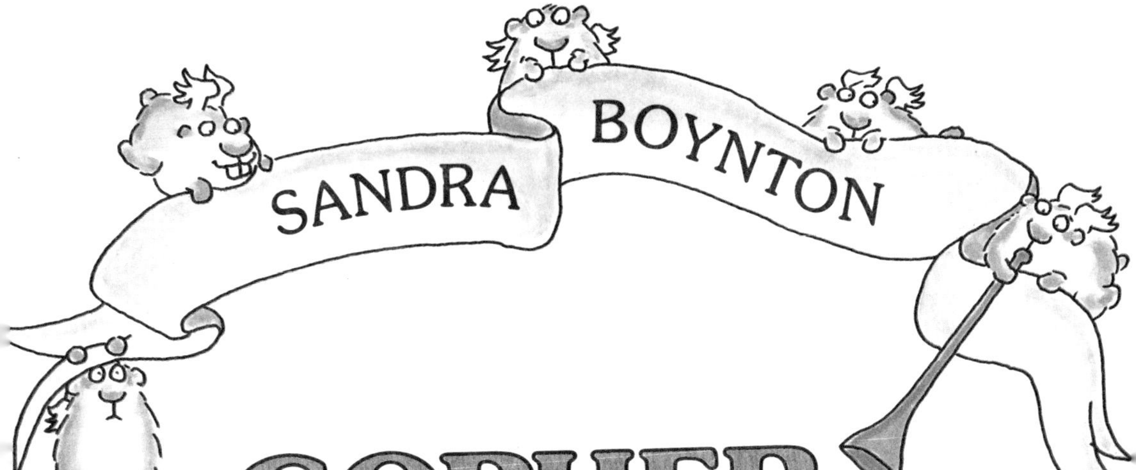
SANDRA
BOYNTON

GOPHER BAROQUE

AND OTHER BEASTLY CONCEITS

Thomas Congdon Books
E.P. DUTTON • NEW YORK

For information contact: E.P. Dutton, 2 Park Avenue, New York, N.Y. 10016

Library of Congress Catalog Card Number: 79-64328

ISBN: 0-525-11585-4 (cloth)
      0-525-03469-2 (paper)

Published simultaneously in Canada by Clarke, Irwin & Company Limited, Toronto and Vancouver

10 9 8 7 6 5 4 3 2 1   First Edition

For My Father

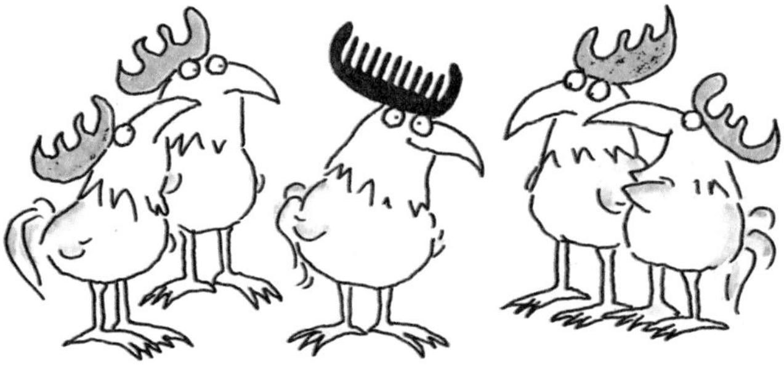

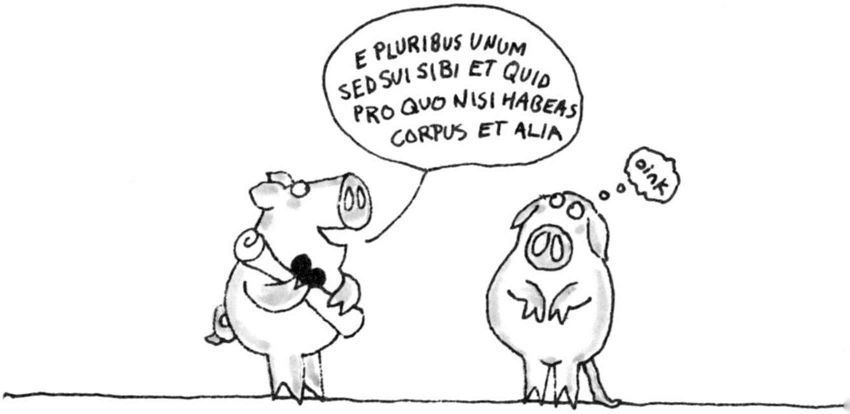
E PLURIBUS UNUM SED SUI SIBI ET QUID PRO QUO NISI HABEAS CORPUS ET ALIA
oink

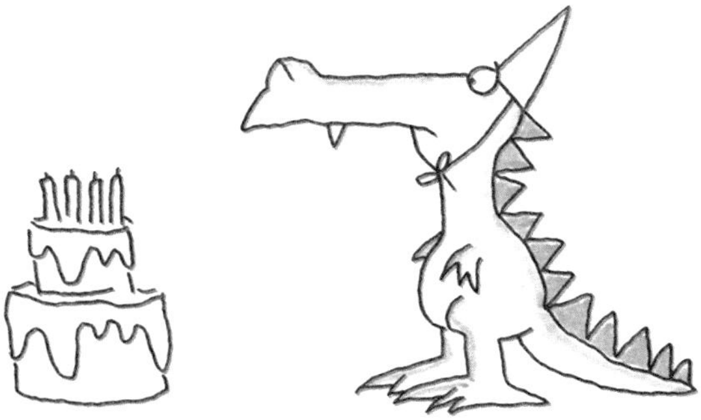

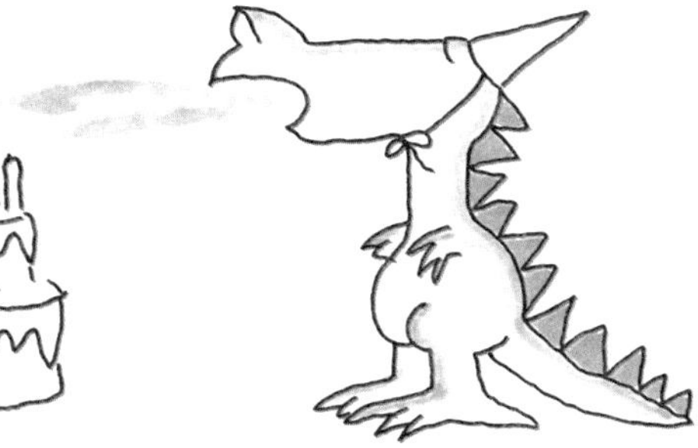

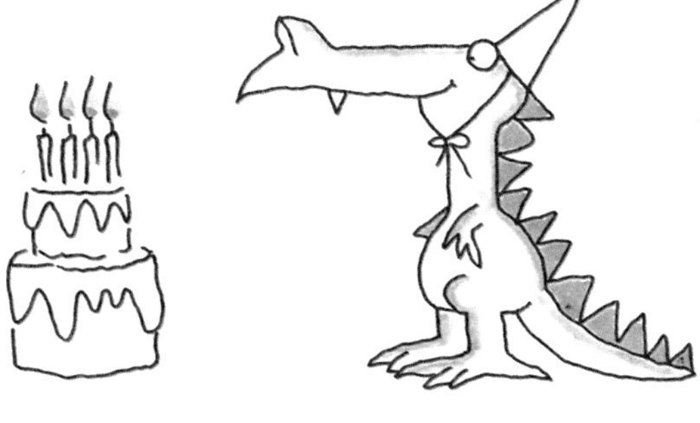

RATS.

HOGWASH.

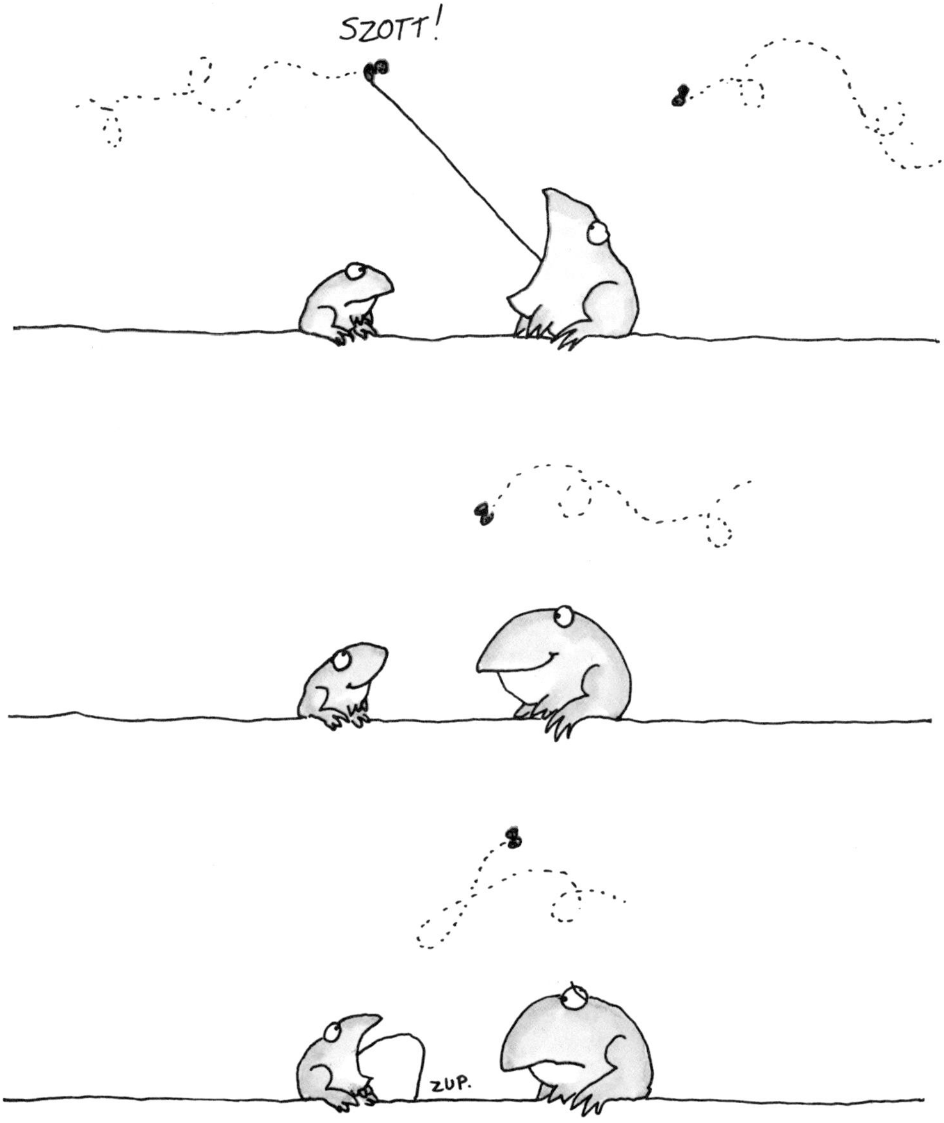
SZOTT!
ZUP.

CRYSTAL

BONE CHINA

HIPPSCOTCH

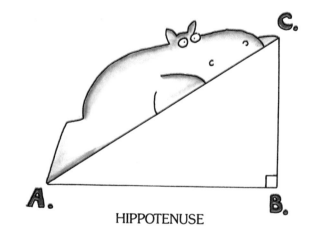

HIPPOTENUSE

HIPPOCRITICAL

CLEHIPPATRA

HIPPO-GO-LUCKY

HIPPOCHONDRIAC

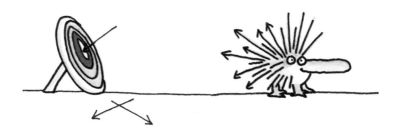

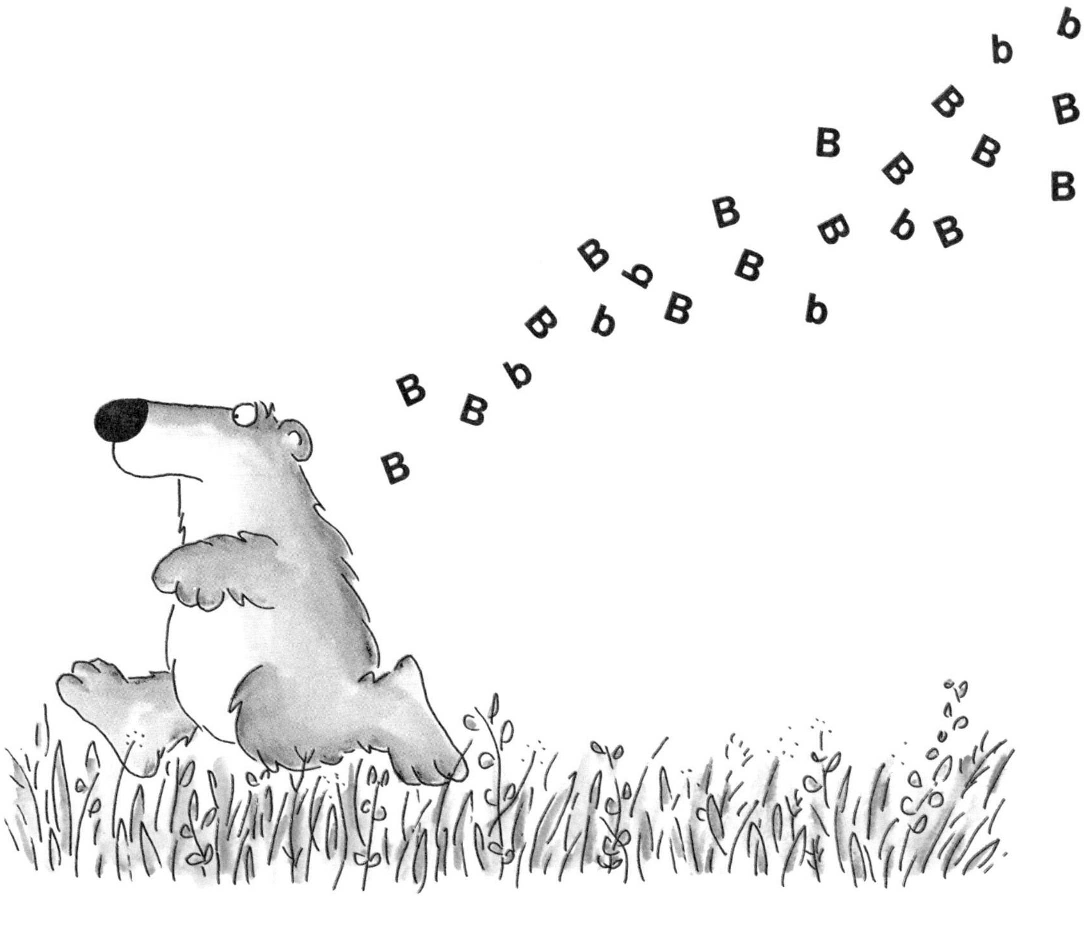

"Someday, Kid, all this will be yours."

"Quack."

ARRESTING PERSONALITY

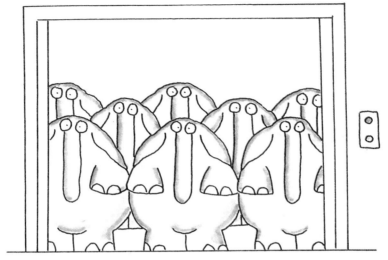

ELEPHATOR

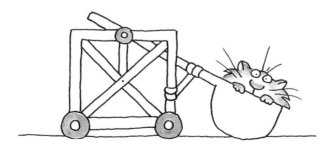

CATAPULT

Never say diet.

DUCK!—

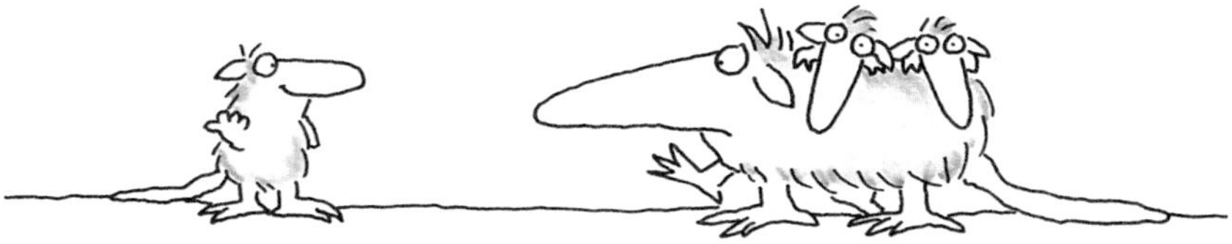

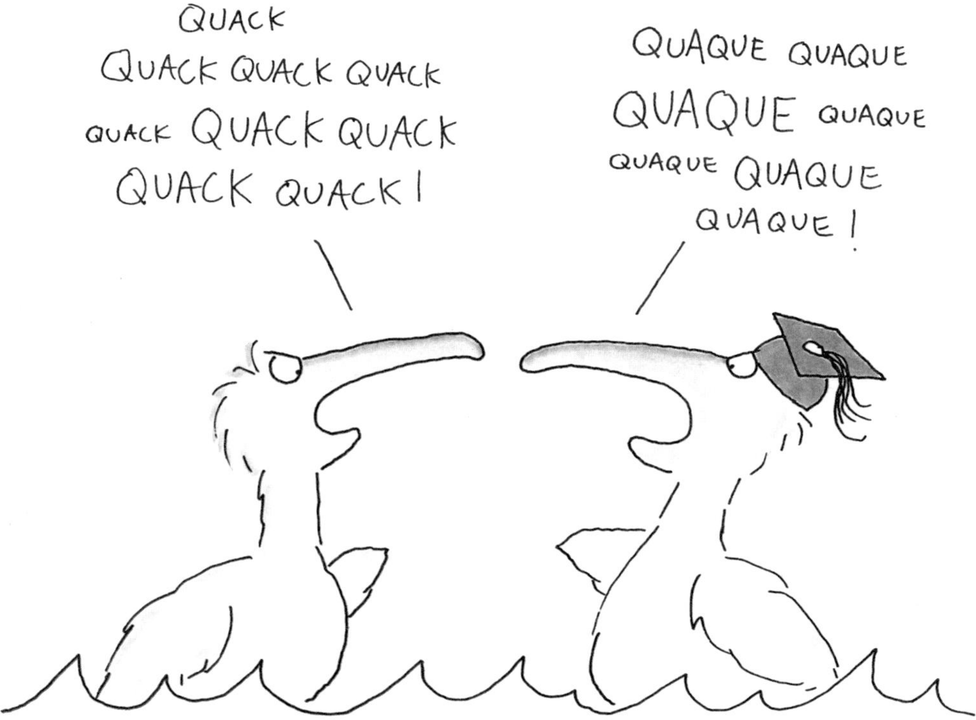
QUACK
QUACK QUACK QUACK
QUACK QUACK QUACK
QUACK QUACK!
QUAQUE QUAQUE
QUAQUE QUAQUE
QUAQUE QUAQUE
QUAQUE!

TOUCAN TANGO

21-BUN SALUTE

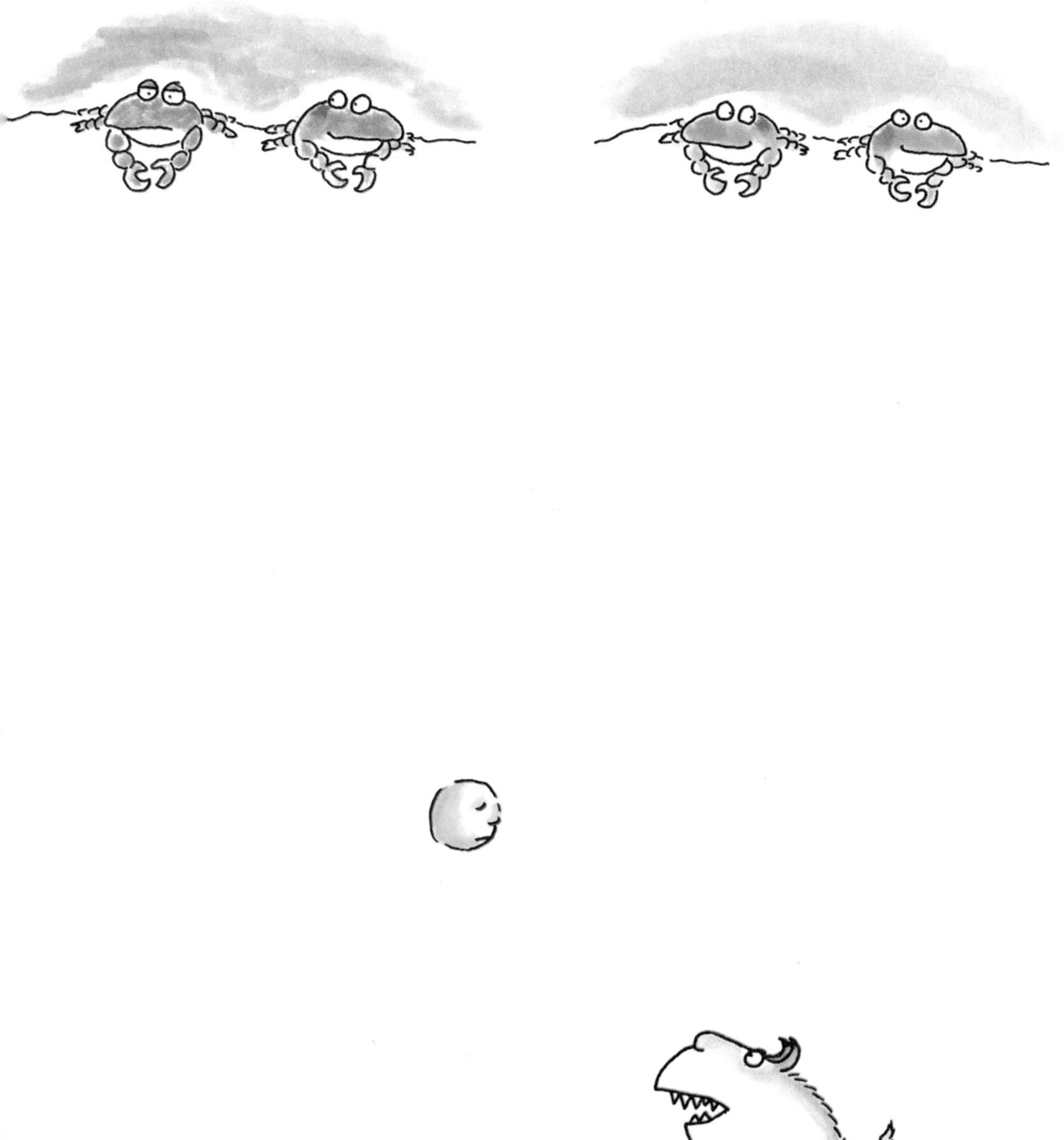

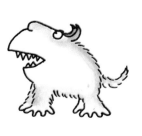

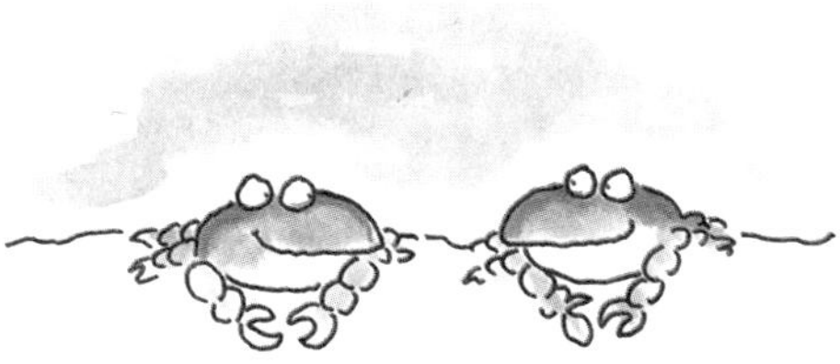

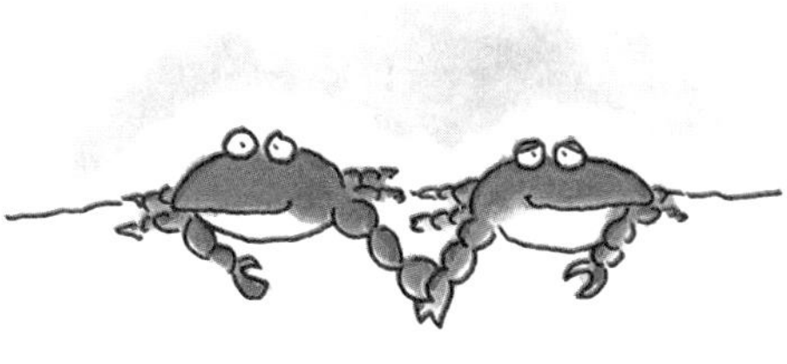

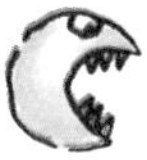

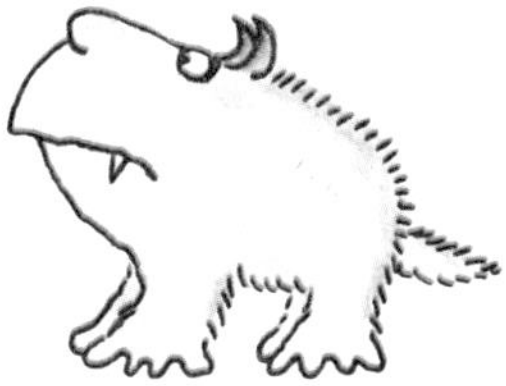

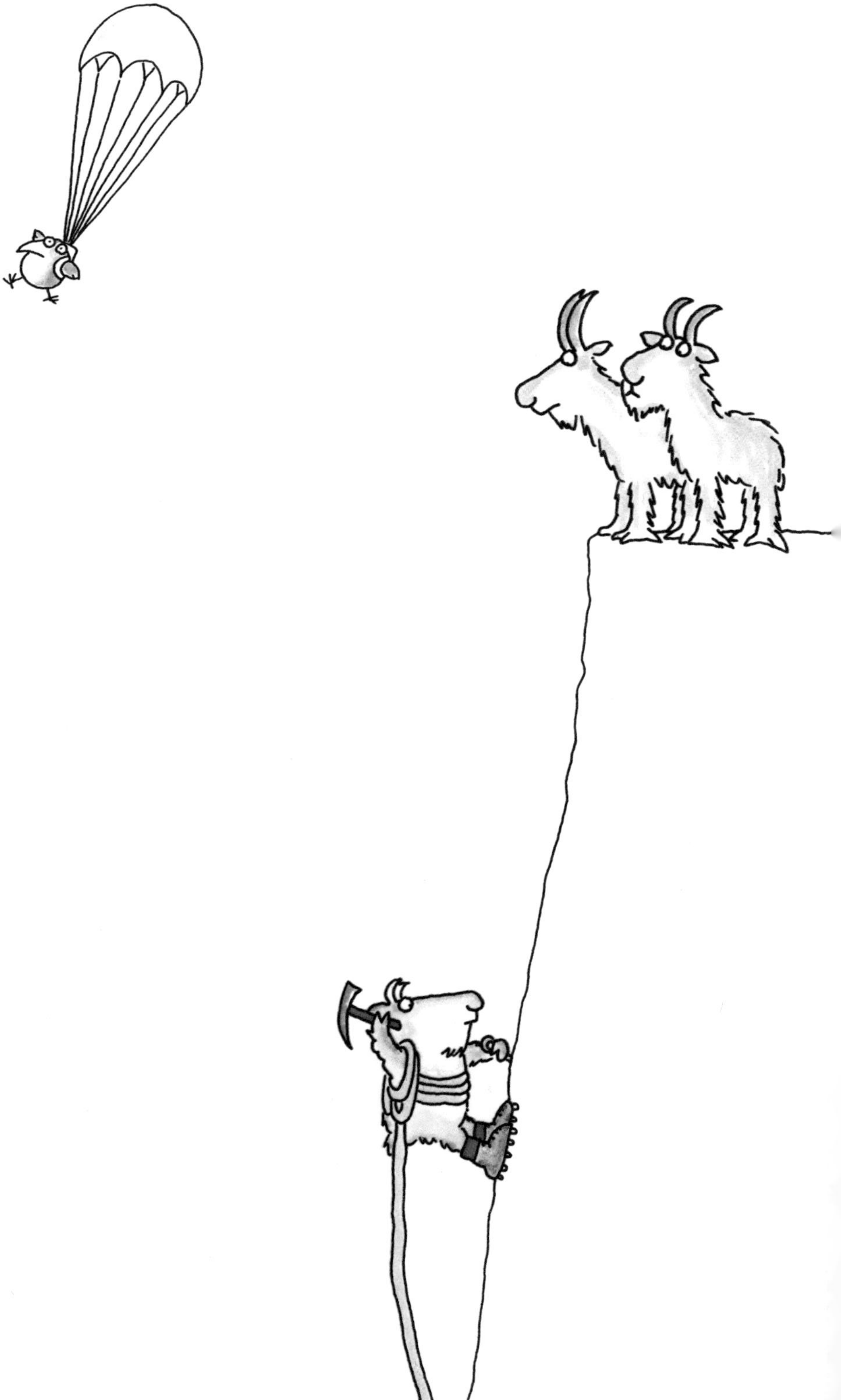

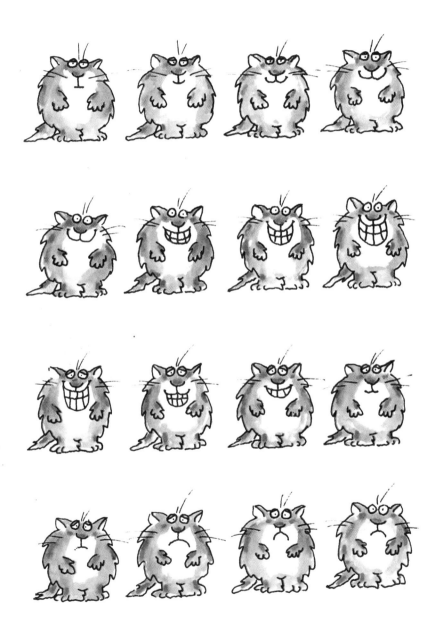

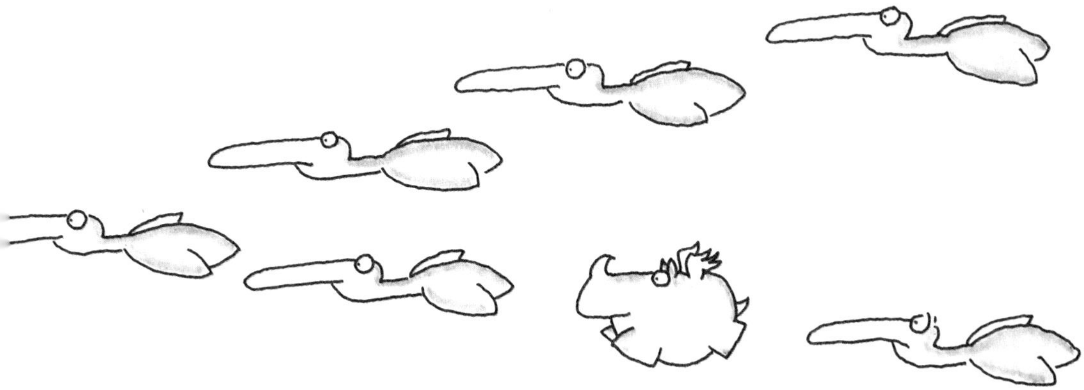

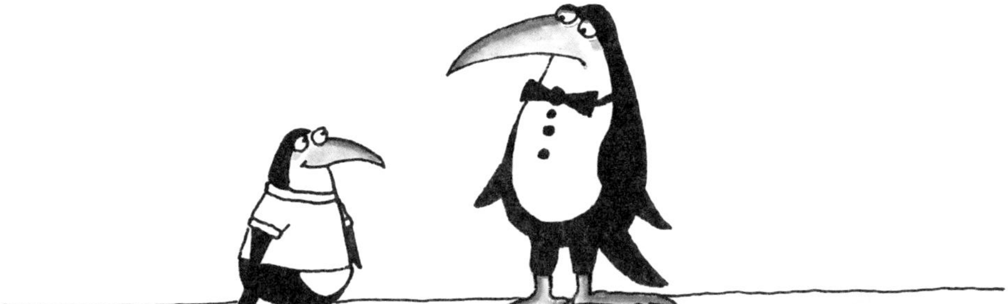

TEAM

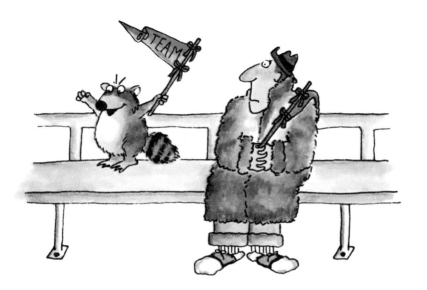

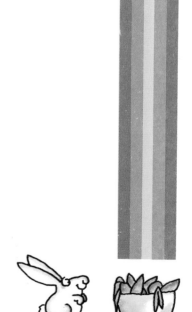

GOBBLE
GOBBLE GOBBLE
GOBBLE GOBBLE GOBBLE
GOBBLE GOBBLE
GOBBLE GOBBLE
GOBBLE GOBBLE
GOBBLE GOBBLE

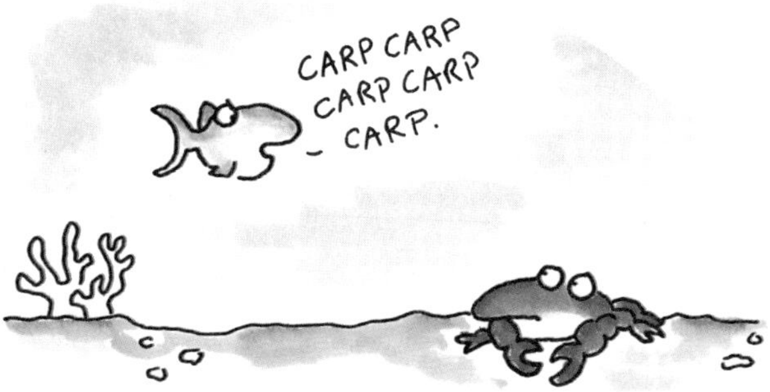
CARP CARP
CARP CARP
CARP.

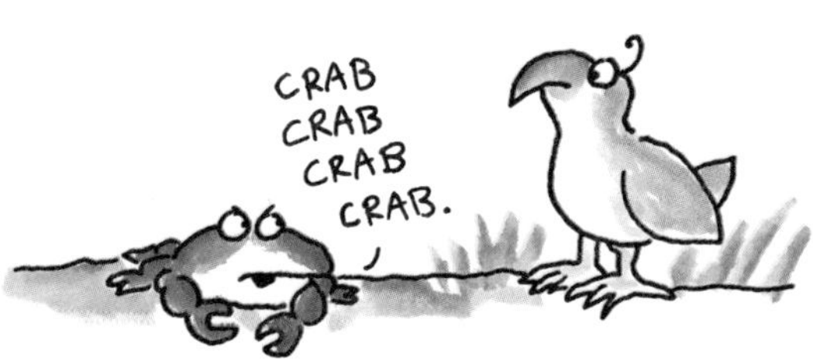
CRAB
CRAB
CRAB
CRAB.

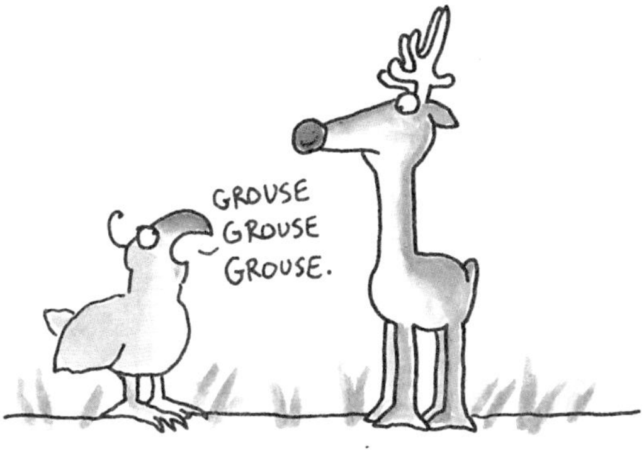
GROUSE
GROUSE
GROUSE.

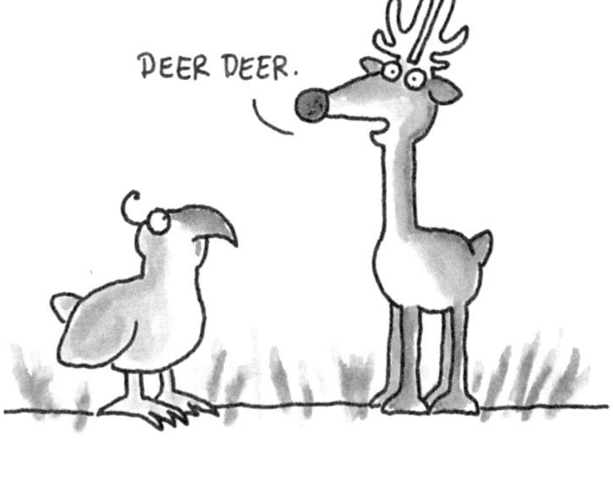
DEER DEER.

LION OF LEAST RESISTANCE

"Moo, moo, moo, that's all I ever hear."

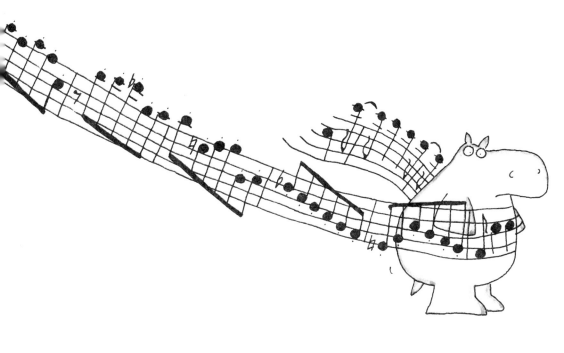

ABSOLUTE BOAR

BUREAUCRAT

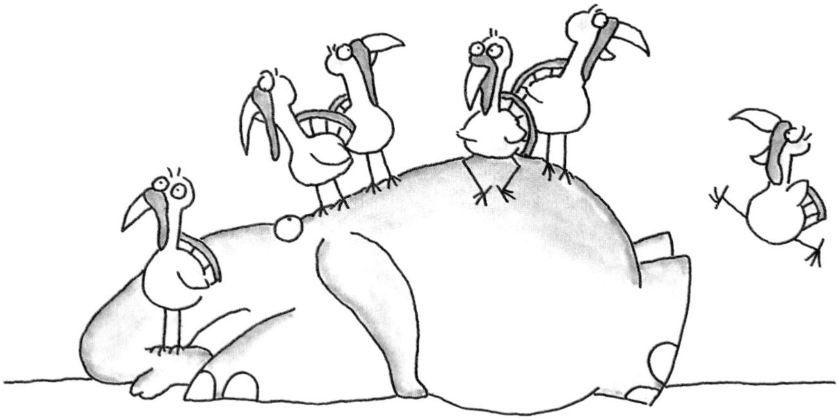

Don't let the turkeys get you down.

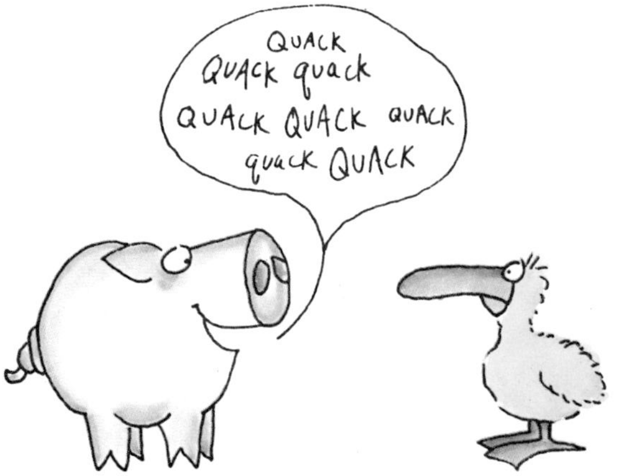
QUACK
QUACK quack
QUACK QUACK QUACK
quack QUACK

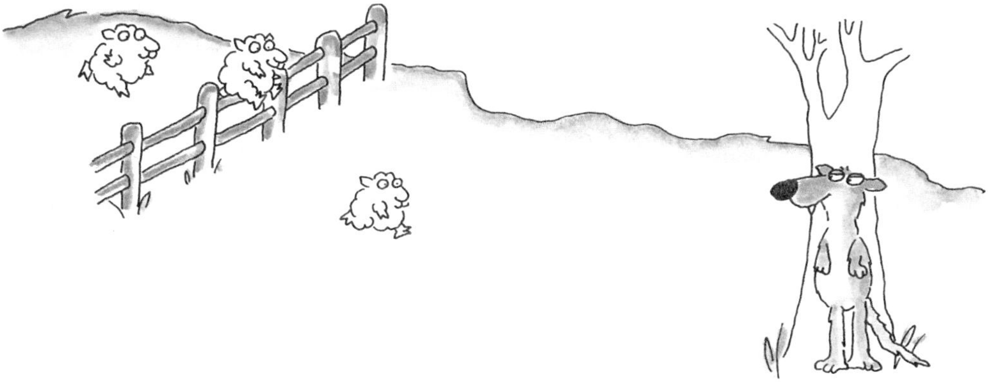
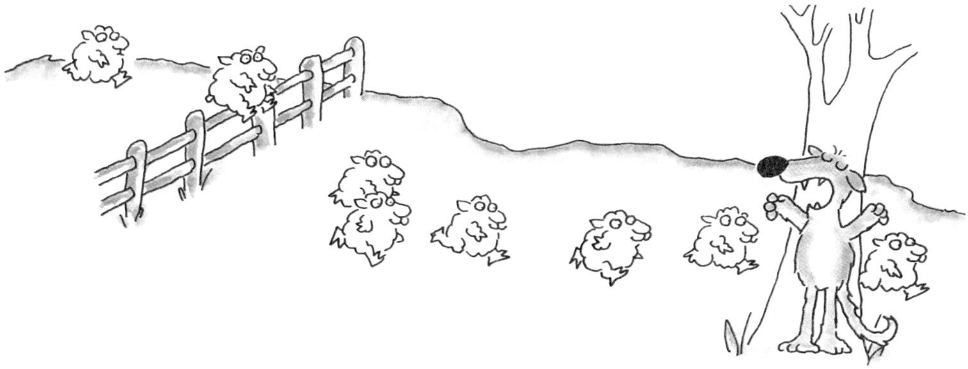
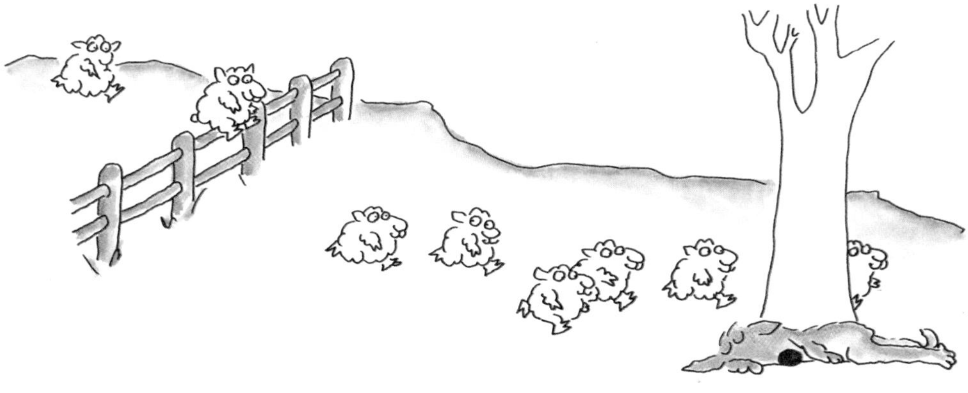

Have Faith.

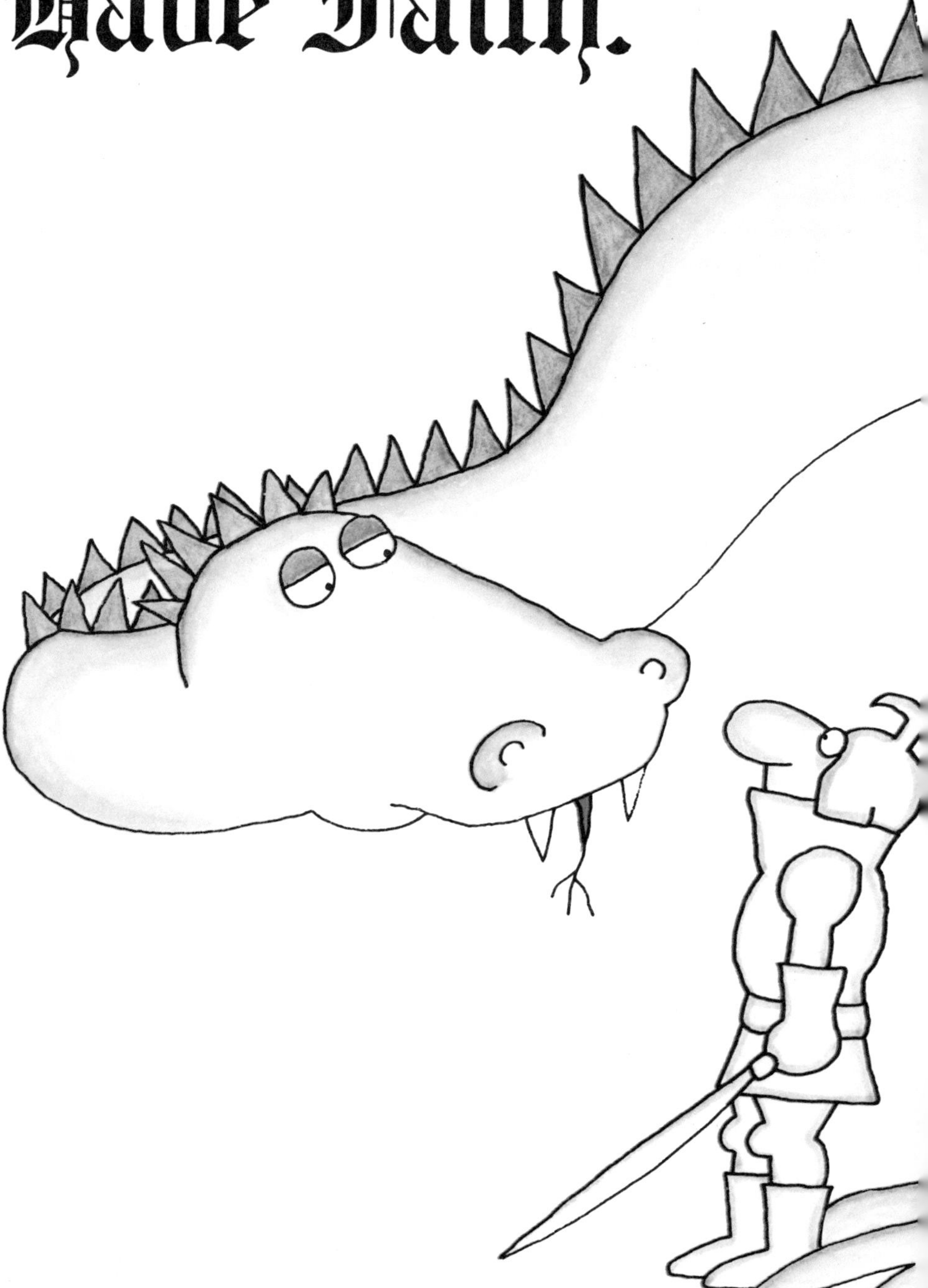

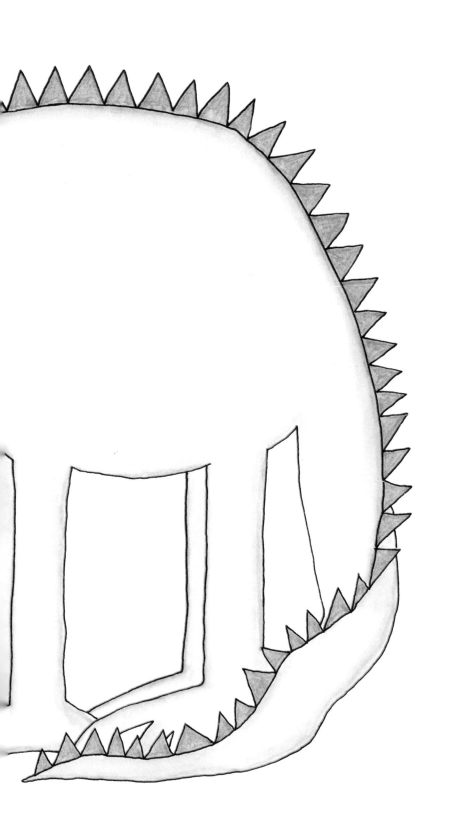

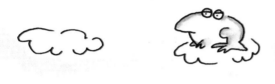

DELUPP.

BAROOOK
BAROOOK!

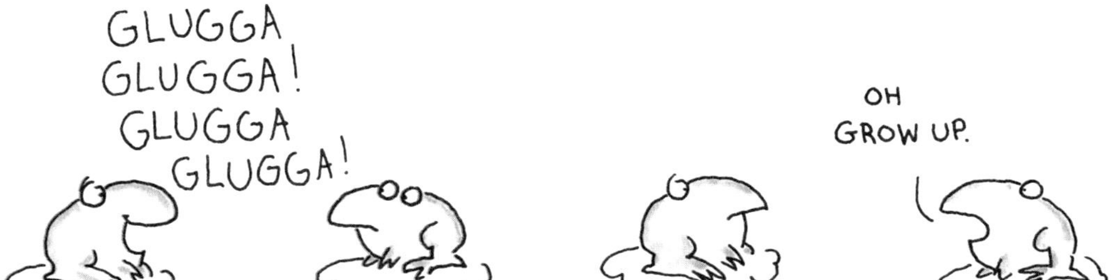
GLUGGA
GLUGGA!
GLUGGA
GLUGGA!
OH
GROW UP.

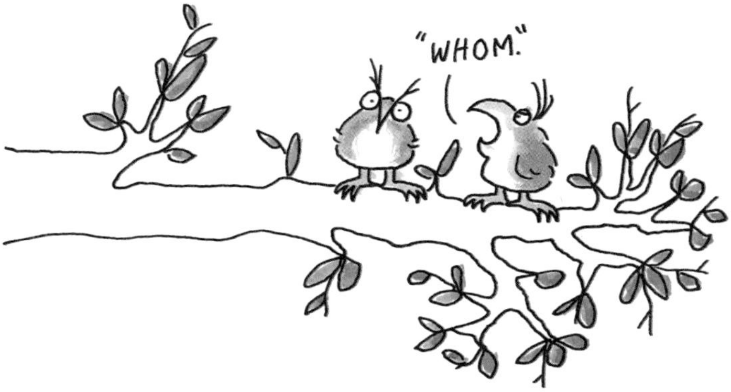
"WHOM."

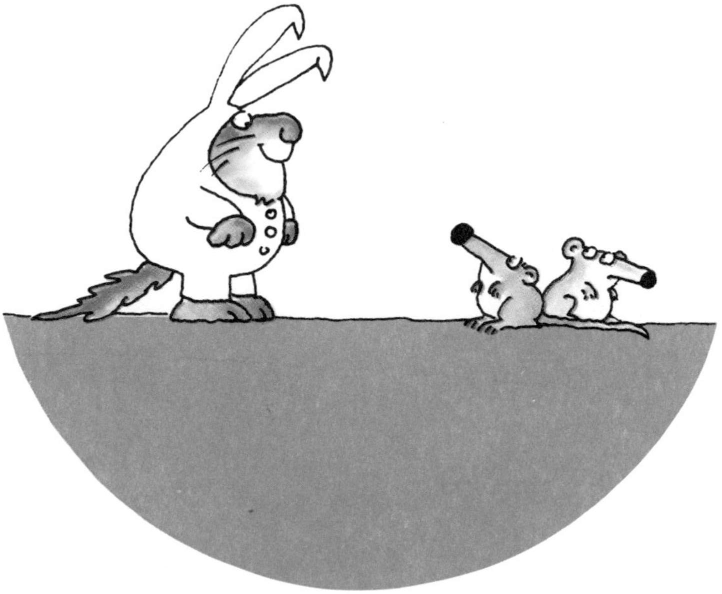

O, who is writing poetry sublime?

I amb, I amb, I amb, I amb, I amb.

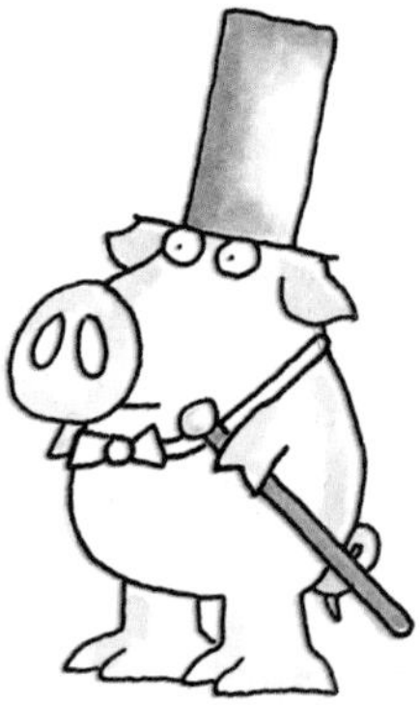

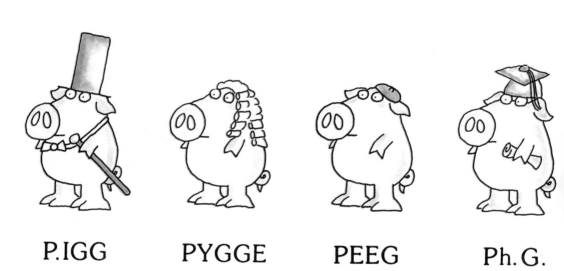

P.IGG

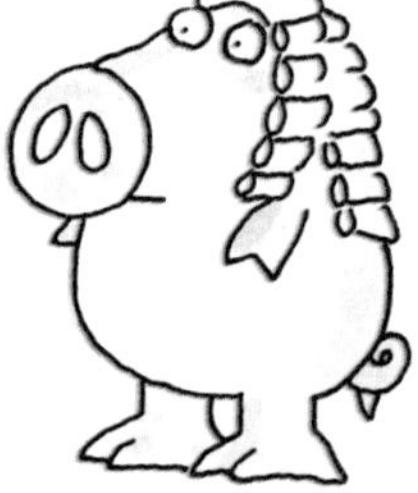

PYGGE

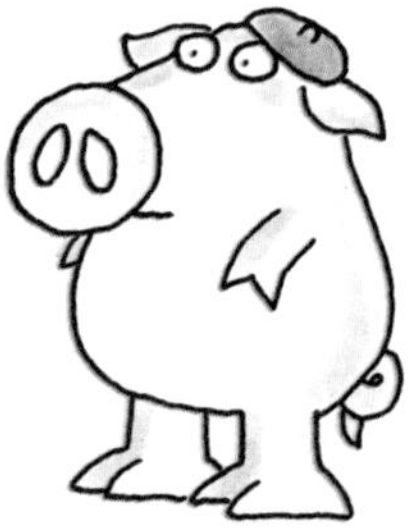

PEEG

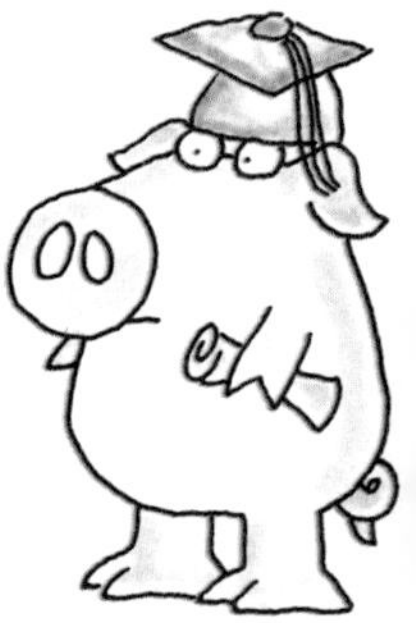

Ph. G.

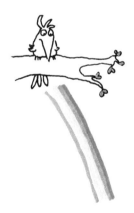

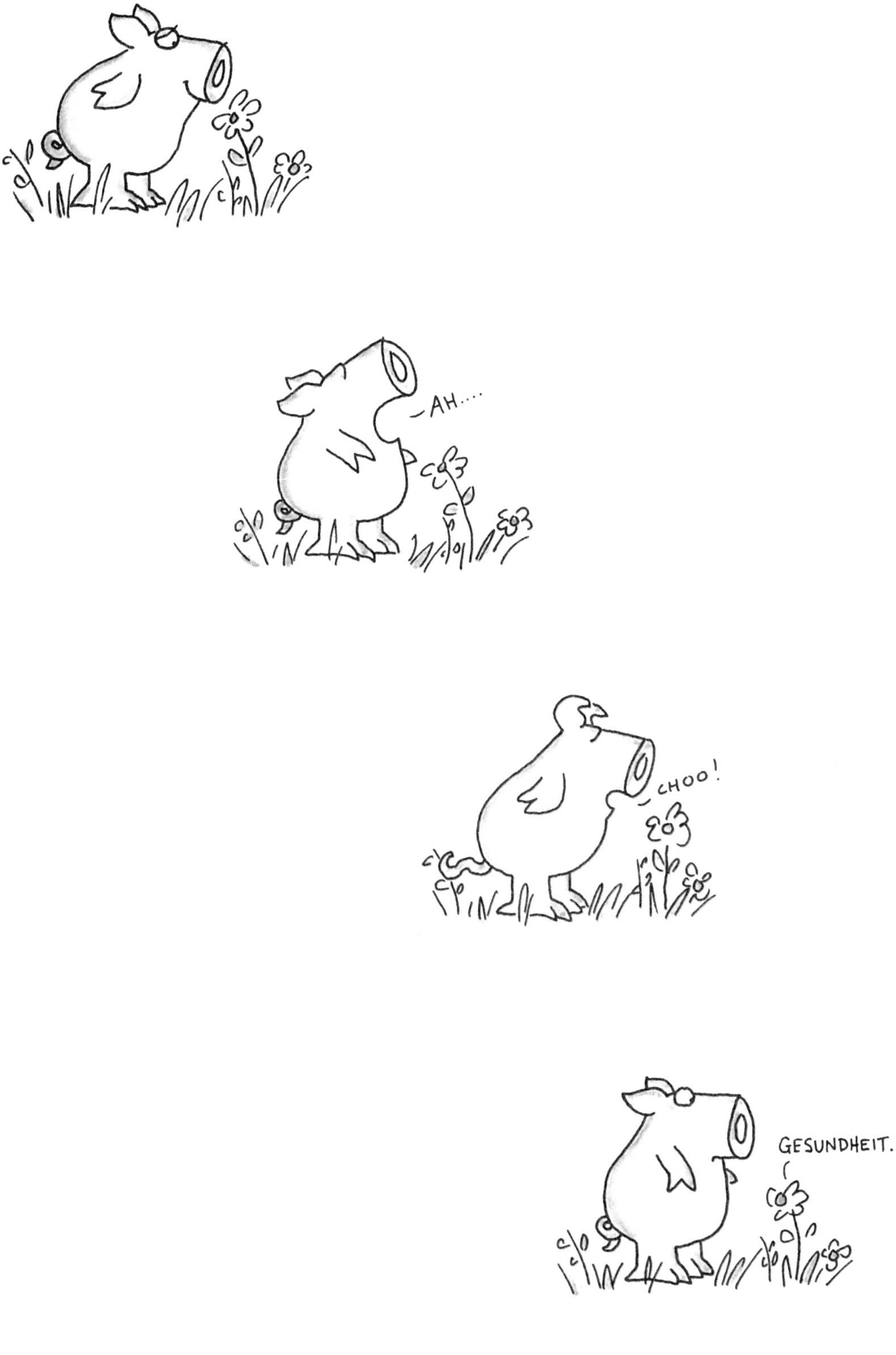
AH....
CHOO!
GESUNDHEIT.

DO-IT-YOURSELF TURKEY KIT

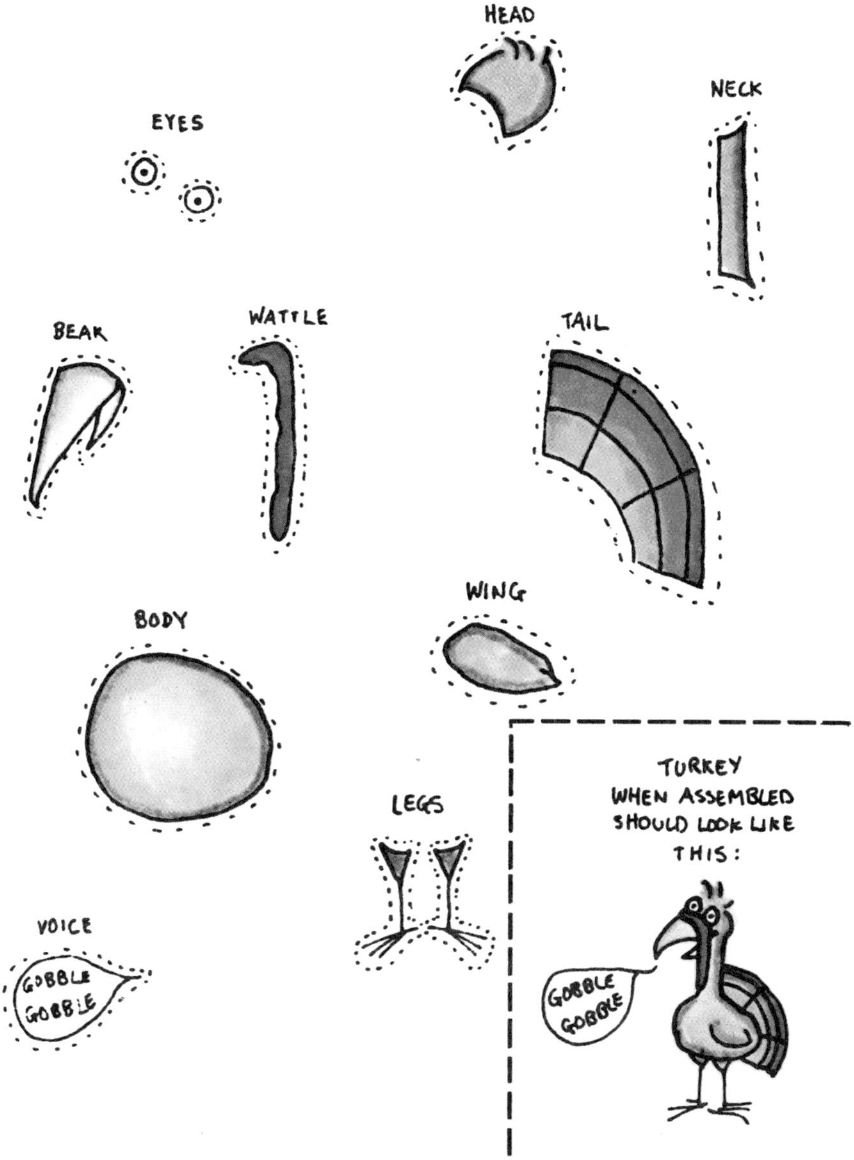
HEAD
NECK
EYES
BEAK
WATTLE
TAIL
WING
BODY
LEGS
VOICE
GOBBLE GOBBLE
TURKEY WHEN ASSEMBLED SHOULD LOOK LIKE THIS:
GOBBLE GOBBLE

HAM

HAMLET

FEELING BEASTLY

"See you later, Alligator."

HIPPO   BIRDIE   TWO EWES

HIPPO BIRDIE   TWO EWES

HIPPO   BIRDIE   DEER   EWE

HIP-PO BIR-DIE TWO EWES!

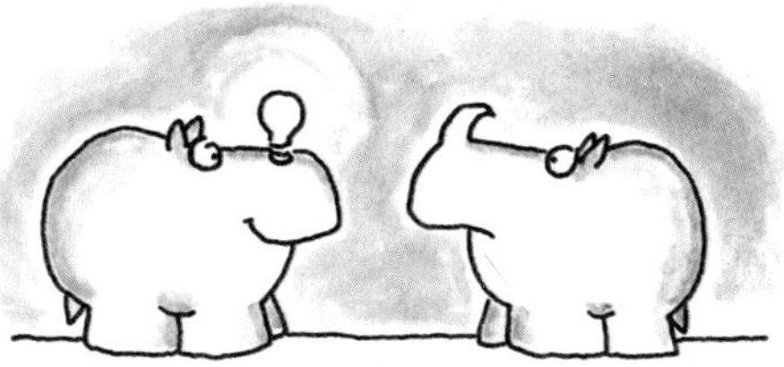

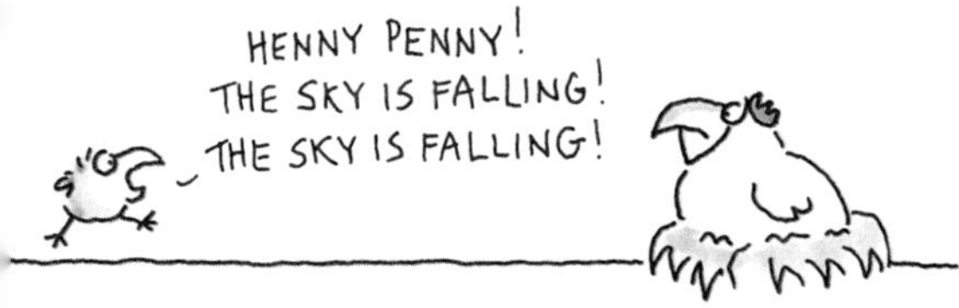
HENNY PENNY!
THE SKY IS FALLING!
THE SKY IS FALLING!

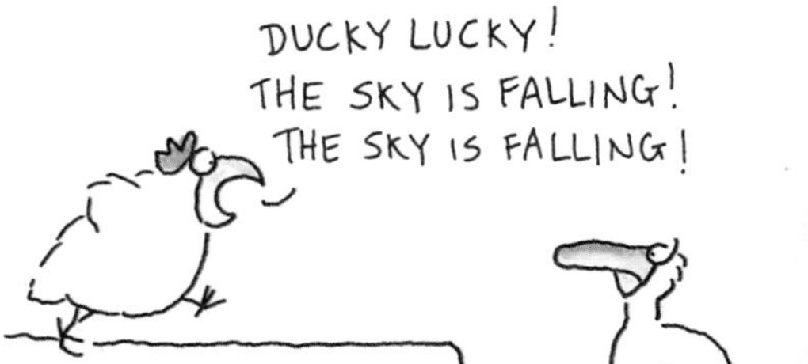
DUCKY LUCKY!
THE SKY IS FALLING!
THE SKY IS FALLING!

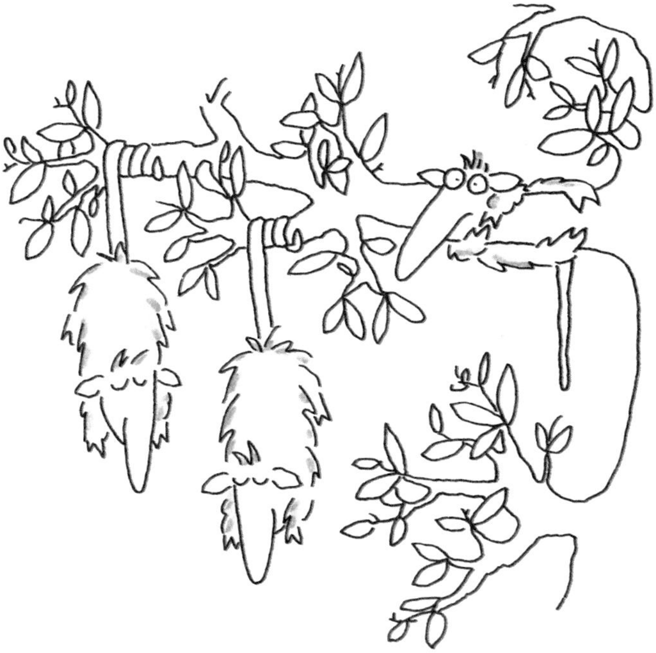

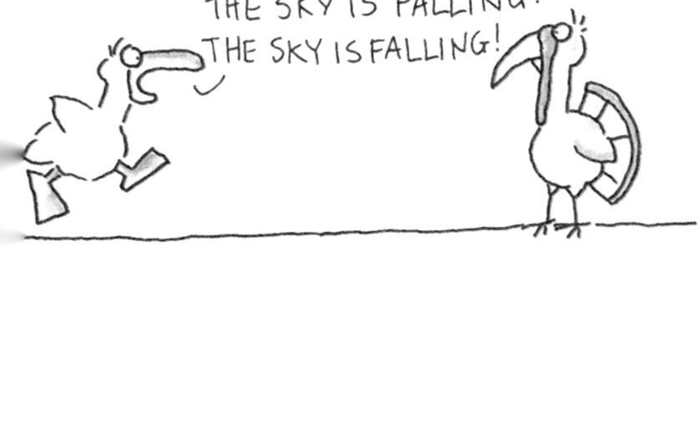
TURKEY LURKEY!
THE SKY IS FALLING!
THE SKY IS FALLING!

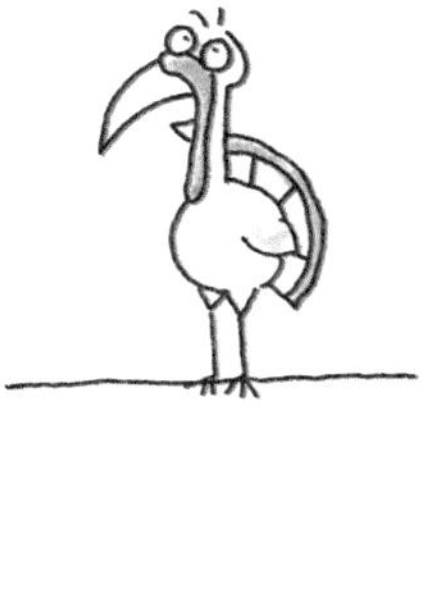
LET'S SEE NOW:
WHO COMES AFTER
TURKEY LURKEY?

You are you,
and I am I.
We are alone, together.
And if the I that is I
is not in harmony with
the you that is you,
then the we that is us
will become the them that was,
or were.

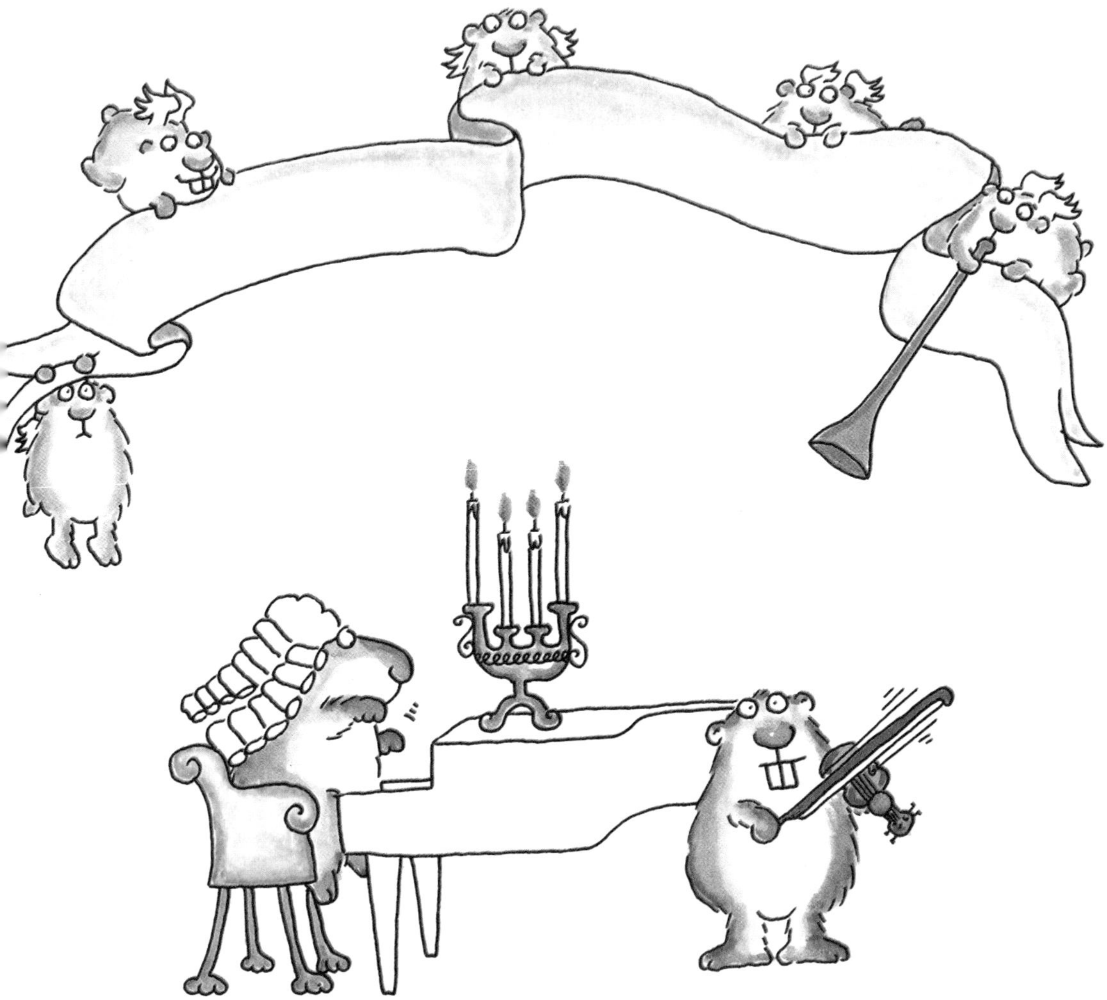

GOPHER BAROQUE

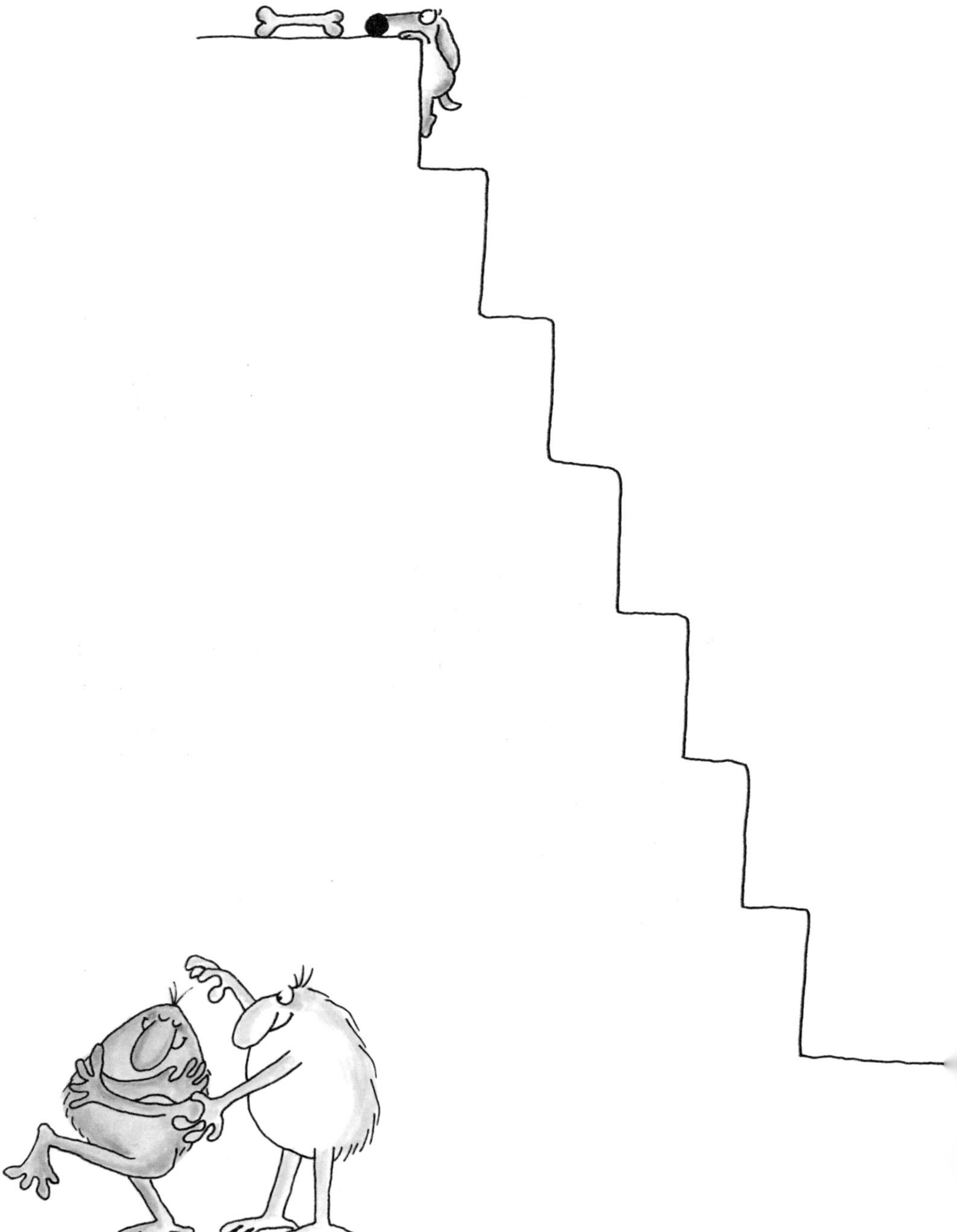

TICKLED PINK

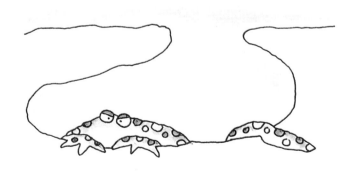

HARBORED GRUDGE

PAS DE DEUX

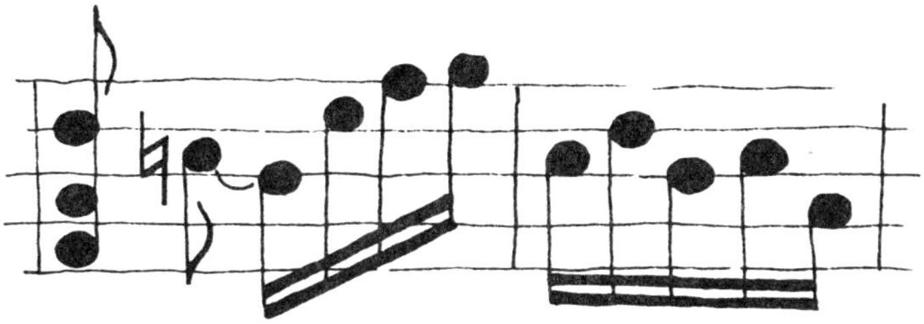

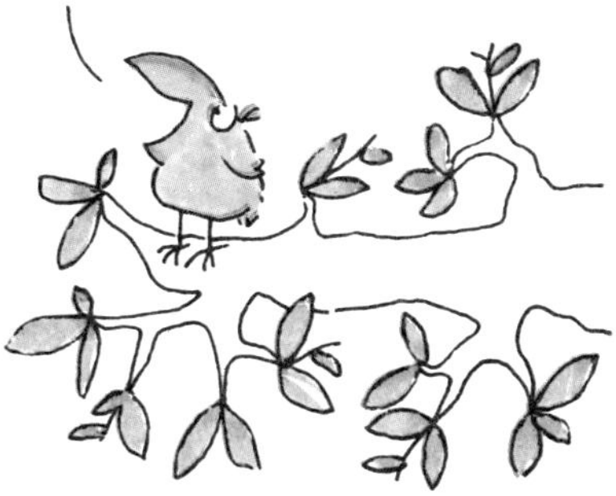

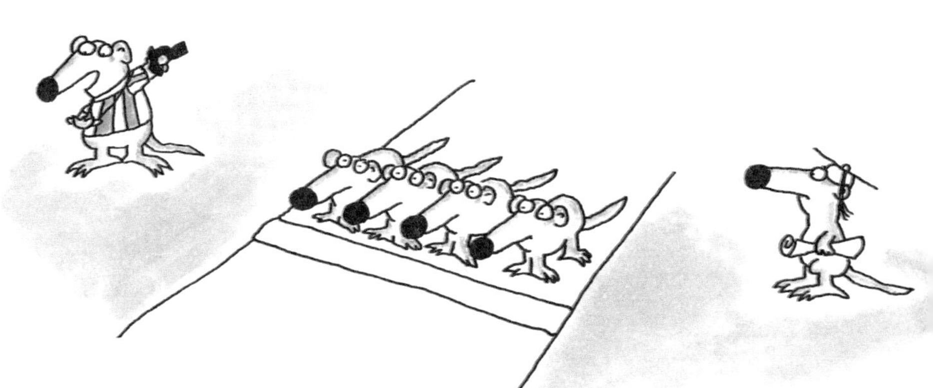

BLANK CHICK

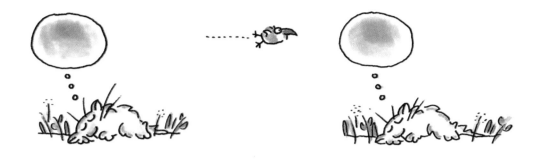

"I pledge thee my trough."

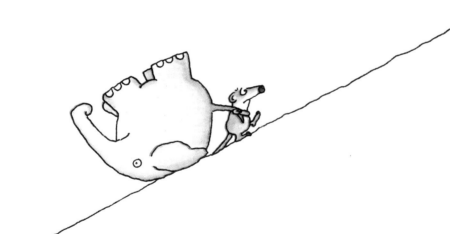

Into each life, a little rain must fall.

Believe in yourself.

Today is the first day
of the rest of your life.

Let a smile be your umbrella.

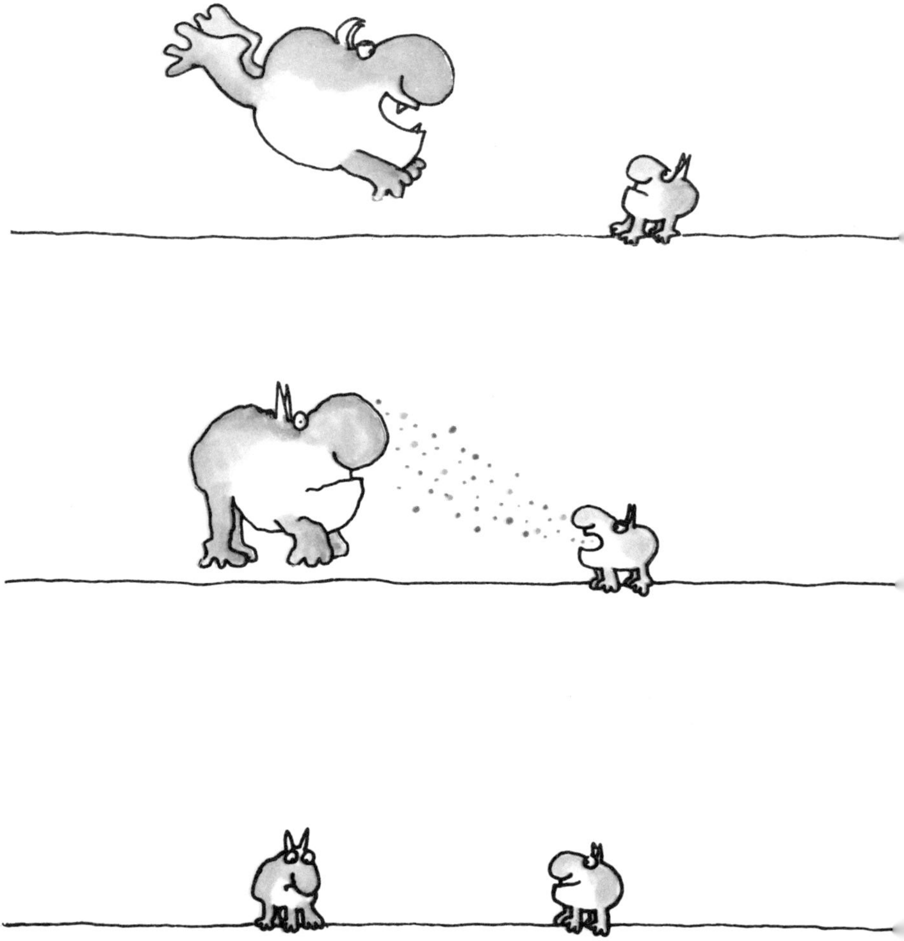

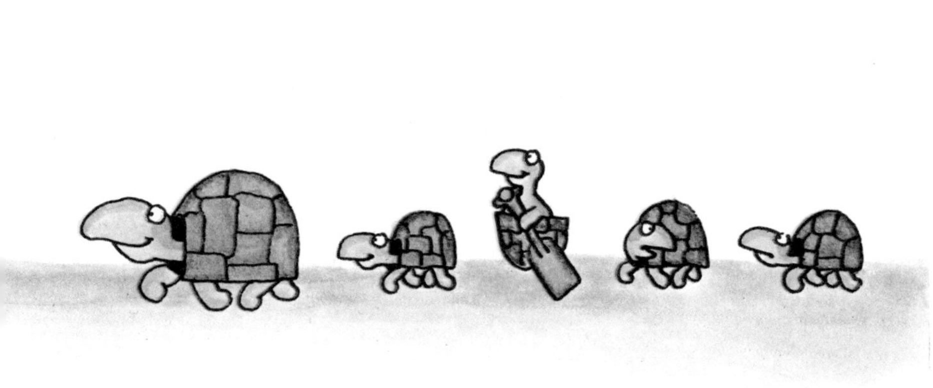

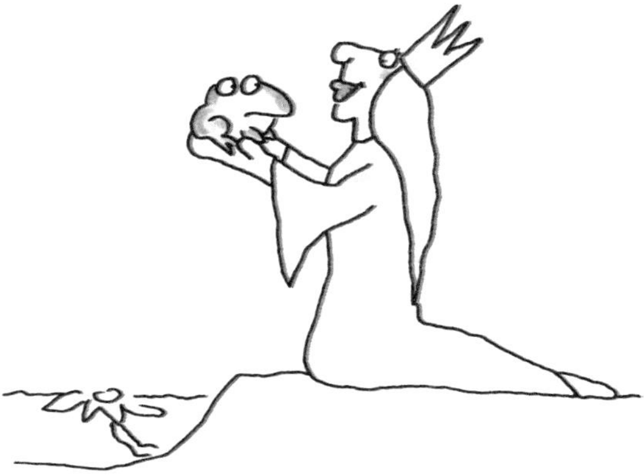

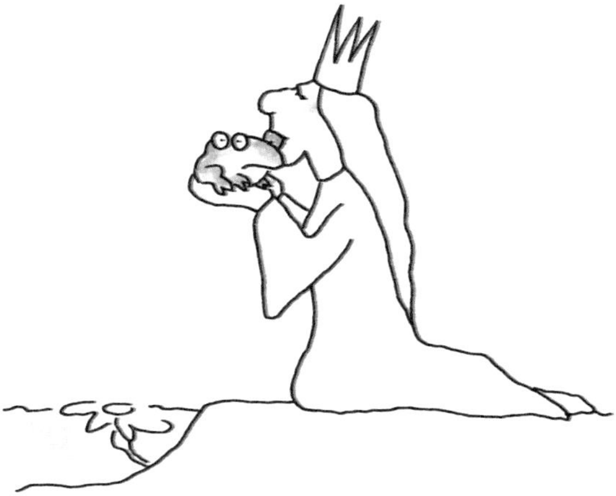

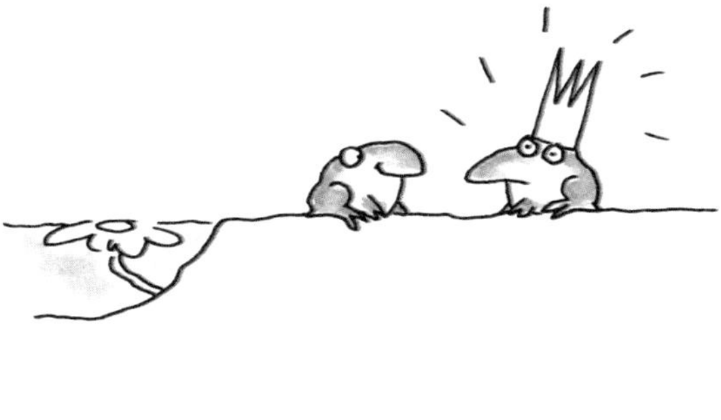

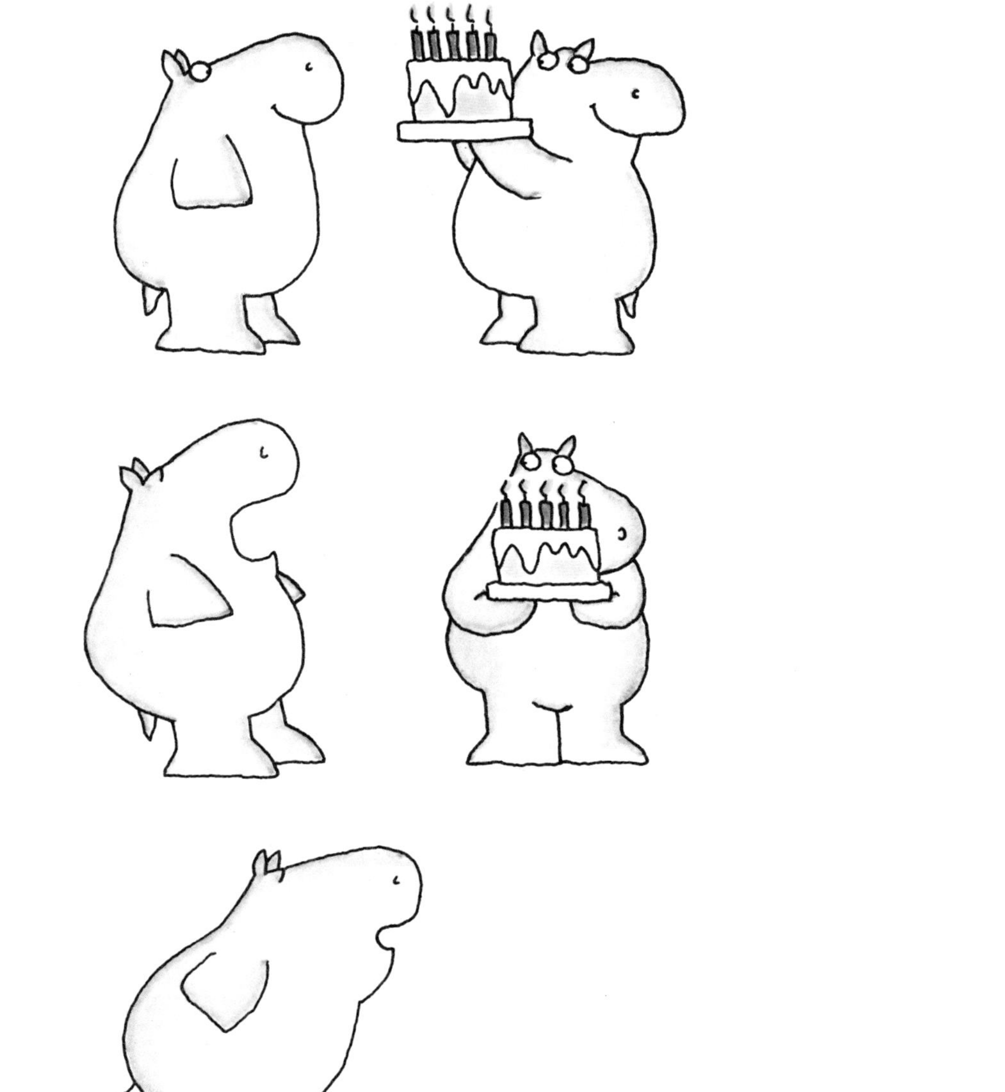

If a being
does not keep pace
with its companions,
perhaps it is because
it hears a
different drummer.
Or maybe it's just a weirdo.

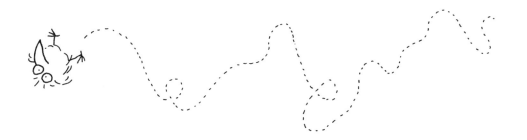

"Kiss me, you fool."

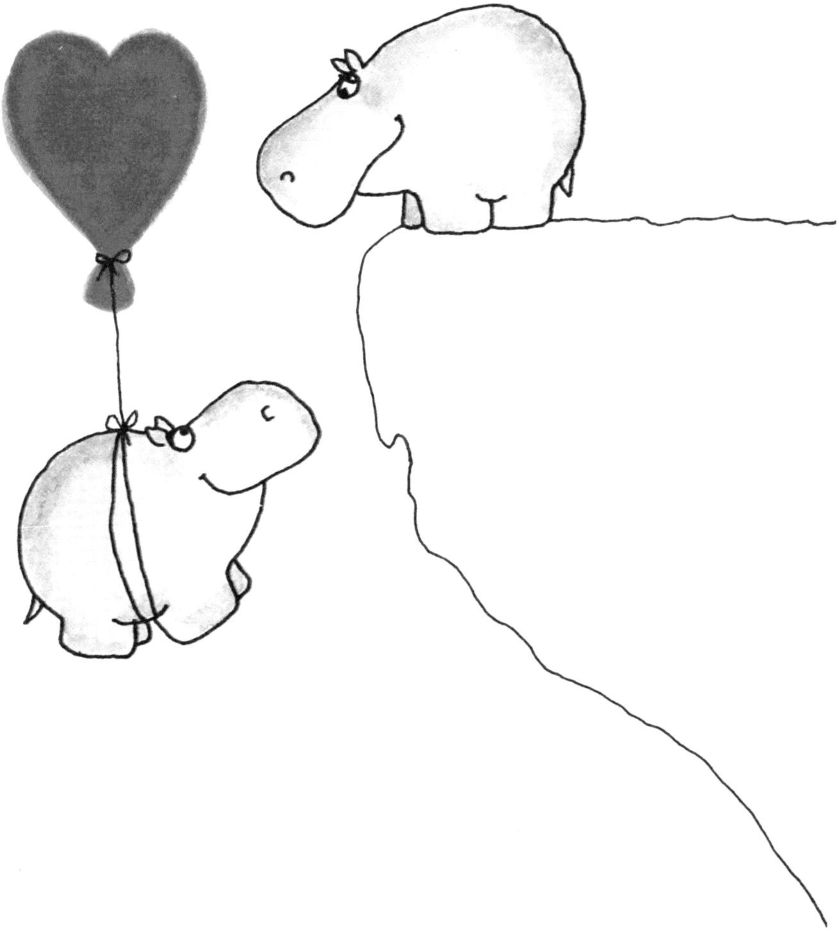

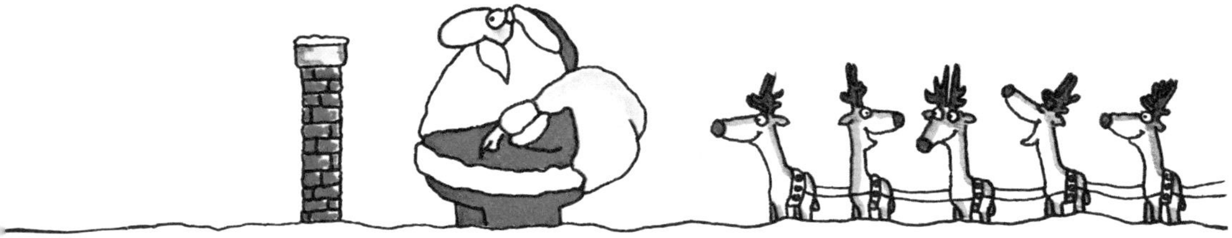

"Dam, dam, dam."

"If you're so smart, how come you aren't rich?"

MOOSLE

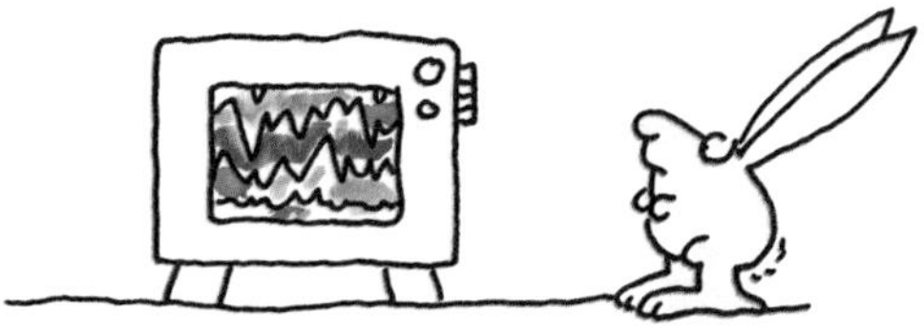

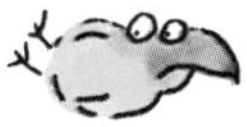

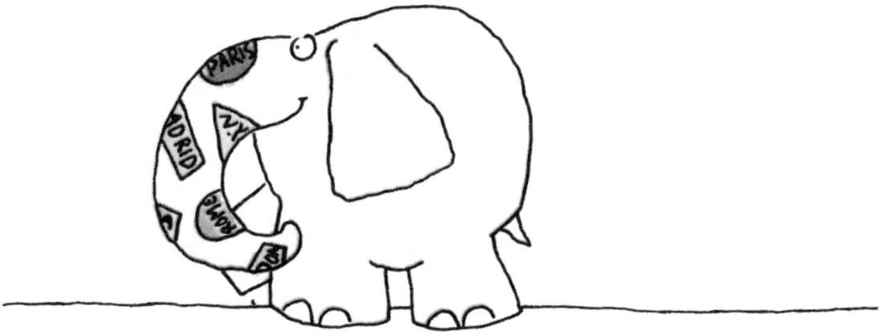
PARIS
ADRID
N.Y.

Whoopee!

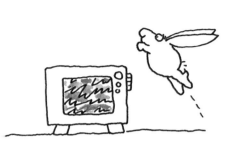

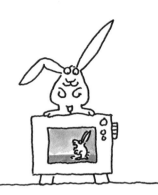

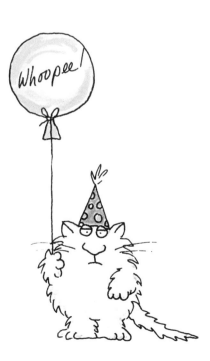

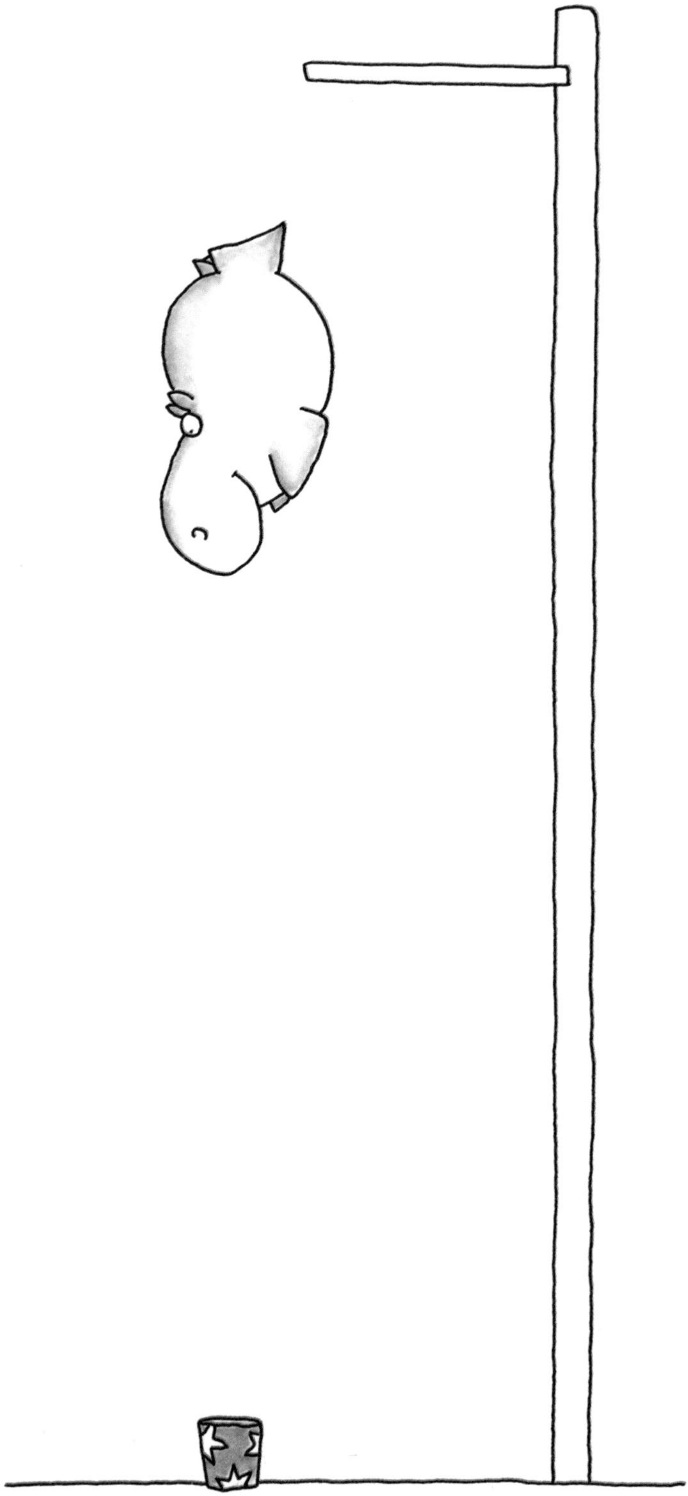

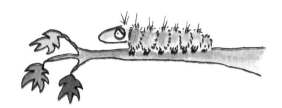

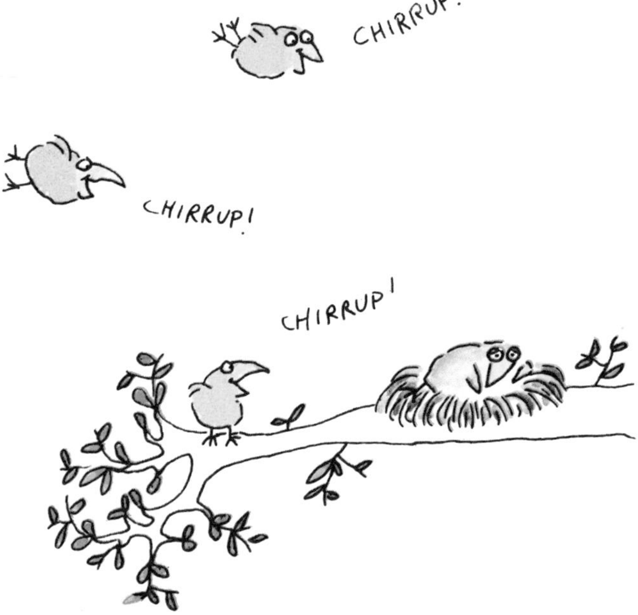
CHIRRUP!
CHIRRUP!
CHIRRUP!

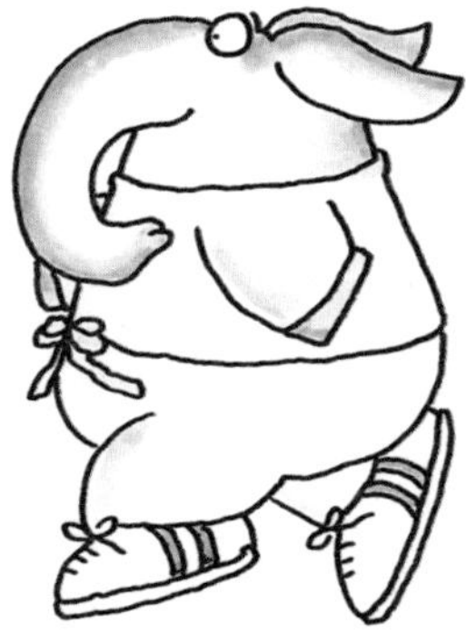

JOGGING THE MEMORY

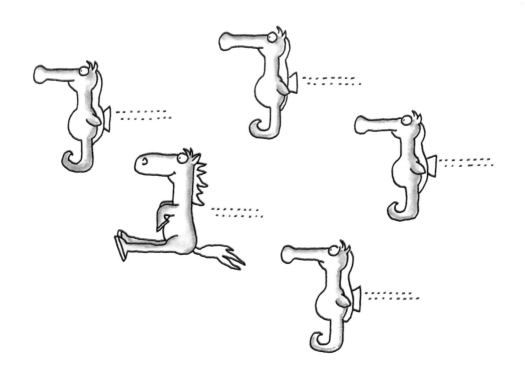